Contents

Answers to the questions are on the back of the Pull-out Poster in the centre of the book.

This book covers unit 3D from the year three scheme of work

Published by Coordination Group Publications Ltd.

Contributors:

Taissa Csáky   Becky May

Chris Dennett   Katherine Reed

Dominic Hall   Claire Thompson

Tim Major   James Paul Wallis

ISBN 1-84146-253-5

Groovy website: www.cgpbooks.co.uk

Jolly bits of clipart from CorelDRAW

Printed by Elanders Hindson, Newcastle upon Tyne.

With thanks to Christine Tinkler and Glenn Rogers for the proof-reading.

Background

I know that rocks aren't the most exciting things in the world.
But we couldn't do without them — and they are <u>really useful</u>.

Q1 Look at the descriptions below and draw lines to match them up with the correct types of rock.

| Very hard and usually white. Can be polished. |

| Grey and quite smooth. Easily splits into thin layers. |

| Light-coloured and very heavy. Rough to touch. |

GRANITE

MARBLE

SLATE

Q2 Write down next to each material whether it's NATURAL or MAN-MADE.

BRICK ....

GRANITE ....

CONCRETE SLAB ....

MARBLE ....

Q3 Bob is building a new home and wants to make sure he uses the best rocks for the job. Look at the types of rock below and write down which he should use for each part of his house.

Roof ....

BRICK

MARBLE   SLATE

Walls ....

Pretty statue in the garden ....

Let's rock and roll...

Not too mind-blowing so far — remember that there are different types of rock that are all used for different things. Don't forget that some are man-made rather than natural.

Grouping Rocks

'Queen' were a rock group... and these are groups of rocks... ha ha ha...

Q1   Sammy has put some pebbles into 2 groups.
He's grouped the pebbles using one of the ways below.
Tick (✓) the correct box to show which way he's used.

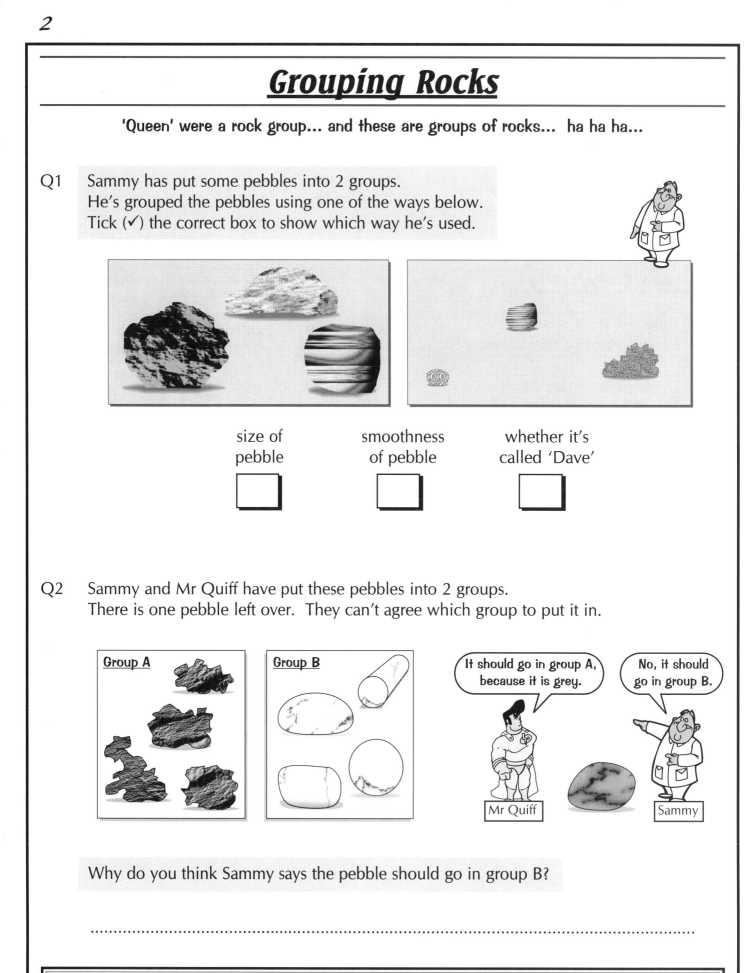

size of
pebble

smoothness
of pebble

whether it's
called 'Dave'

Q2   Sammy and Mr Quiff have put these pebbles into 2 groups.
There is one pebble left over. They can't agree which group to put it in.

Group A

Group B

It should go in group A, because it is grey.

No, it should go in group B.

Mr Quiff

Sammy

Why do you think Sammy says the pebble should go in group B?

....

Have you heard about the shy pebble...

Mmm, lovely rocks... Top Tip — If you get stuck on a 'choose the answer' question
like question 1, just look at each answer one by one and see if it is right or wrong.

Grouping Rocks

More questions about rocks. Fasten your seat belts, these ones are a little more tricky.

Q1   Sammy has put some more pebbles into different groups.

a)   Which way do you think he's grouped the pebbles this time? Tick (✓) the correct box.

size of
particles ☐   shape ☐   size of
pebble ☐

b)   Here is another pebble.
Which group should this pebble go in?
Write 'Group A' or 'Group B'.   ....

Q2   Read this article about sedimentary rocks.

— Sedimentary rocks are made from layers of sand, mud or crushed seashells.
The sand and mud are squashed and squeezed — after *millions of years*
they turn into rock. You can usually see the *layers* in the rock.

— Sedimentary rocks are the only kind of rocks that have *fossils* in them.
Fossils are the remains of dead *plants* and *animals*.

a)   Here are some rocks. Tick (✓) the 2 rocks which you think are sedimentary rocks.

☐   ☐   ☐   ☐

b)   Why did you choose those 2 rocks?

....

....

...it wanted to be a little boulder...

Fossils are brilliant — everything we know about dinosaurs, we know from fossils. Grrr.

Wearing Rocks Away

Some rocks are hard, and some rocks are soft.
...These questions are a bit tricky — read them carefully.

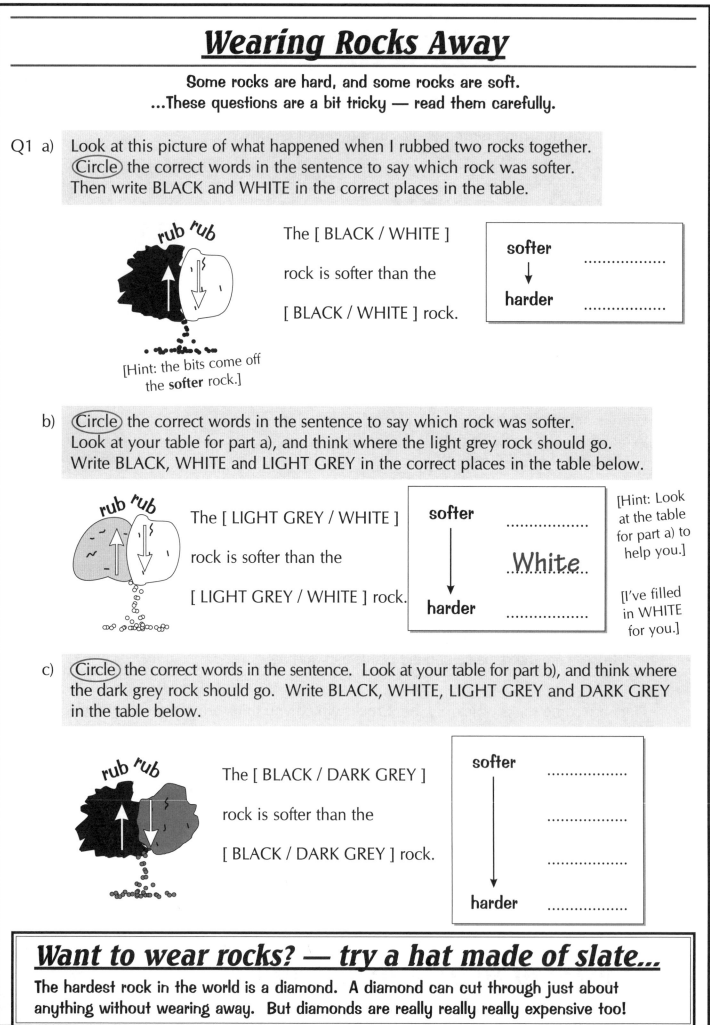

Q1 a) Look at this picture of what happened when I rubbed two rocks together. Circle the correct words in the sentence to say which rock was softer. Then write BLACK and WHITE in the correct places in the table.

The [BLACK / WHITE]

rock is softer than the

[BLACK / WHITE] rock.

softer
↓
harder

[Hint: the bits come off the **softer** rock.]

b) Circle the correct words in the sentence to say which rock was softer. Look at your table for part a), and think where the light grey rock should go. Write BLACK, WHITE and LIGHT GREY in the correct places in the table below.

The [LIGHT GREY / WHITE]

rock is softer than the

[LIGHT GREY / WHITE] rock.

softer
↓
.....White.....
harder

[Hint: Look at the table for part a) to help you.]

[I've filled in WHITE for you.]

c) Circle the correct words in the sentence. Look at your table for part b), and think where the dark grey rock should go. Write BLACK, WHITE, LIGHT GREY and DARK GREY in the table below.

The [BLACK / DARK GREY]

rock is softer than the

[BLACK / DARK GREY] rock.

softer

harder

Want to wear rocks? — try a hat made of slate...

The hardest rock in the world is a diamond. A diamond can cut through just about anything without wearing away. But diamonds are really really really expensive too!

Rocks and Water

One way that rocks can be different from each other is how quickly water soaks in...

Q1   I've done an experiment with rocks and water.
This is what I did:

> 1) Get a rock.
>
> 2) Put a 10 ml amount of water on the rock.
>
> 3) Time how long it takes for all of the water to soak into the rock.
>
> 4) Do the same thing for three more rocks.

You can't test the rocks if your monster eats them all.

This is what happened.

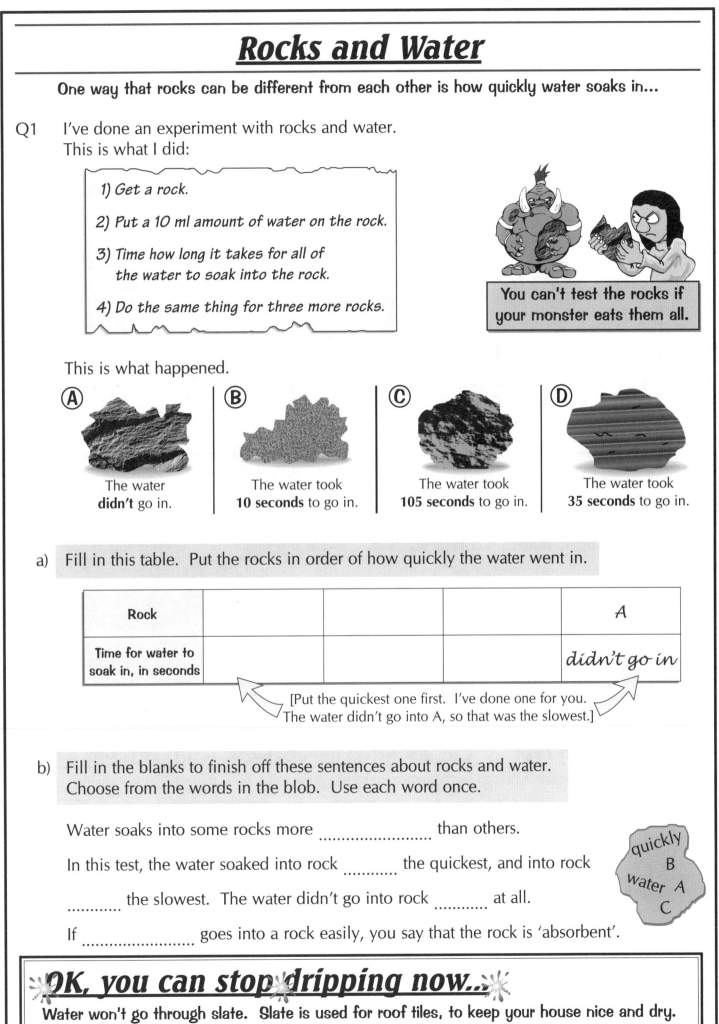

Ⓐ The water **didn't** go in.

Ⓑ The water took **10 seconds** to go in.

Ⓒ The water took **105 seconds** to go in.

Ⓓ The water took **35 seconds** to go in.

a)   Fill in this table. Put the rocks in order of how quickly the water went in.

Rock				A
Time for water to soak in, in seconds				*didn't go in*

[Put the quickest one first. I've done one for you.
The water didn't go into A, so that was the slowest.]

b)   Fill in the blanks to finish off these sentences about rocks and water.
Choose from the words in the blob. Use each word once.

Water soaks into some rocks more .... than others.

In this test, the water soaked into rock .... the quickest, and into rock ....
.... the slowest. The water didn't go into rock .... at all.

If .... goes into a rock easily, you say that the rock is 'absorbent'.

quickly
B
water   A
C

OK, you can stop dripping now...

Water won't go through slate. Slate is used for roof tiles, to keep your house nice and dry.

Properties of Rocks

You can recognise rocks by their properties — each type of rock is a bit different.

Q1 Oswald looked at the properties of some rocks. Use his notepads to fill in the table.
Tick (✓) the boxes of properties he noticed — don't worry about the ones he didn't spot.

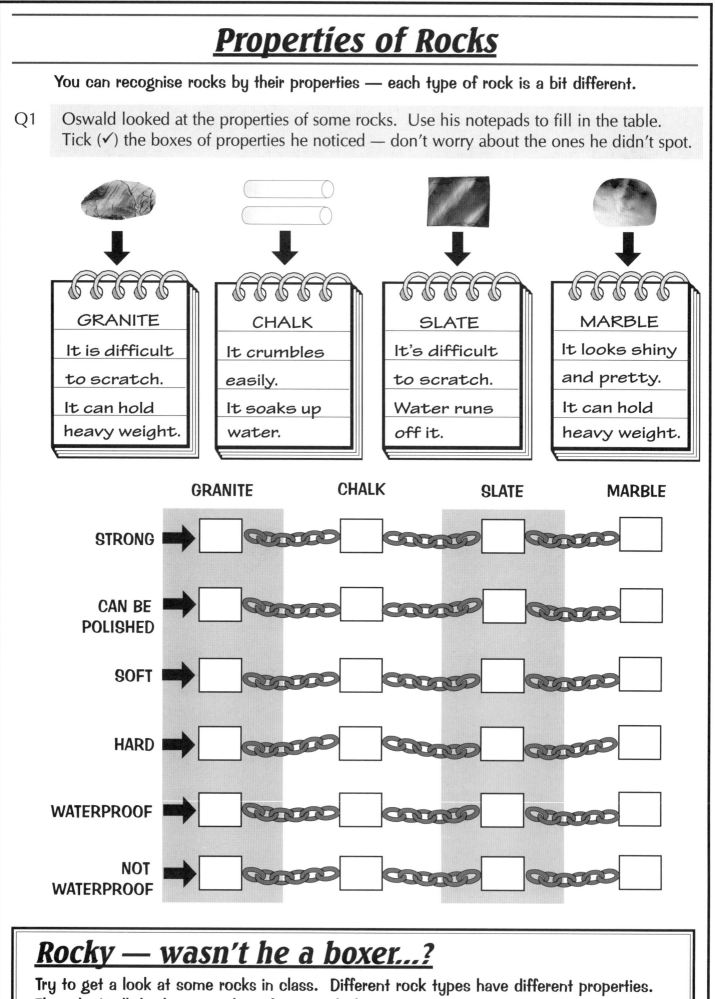

GRANITE

It is difficult to scratch.
It can hold heavy weight.

CHALK

It crumbles easily.
It soaks up water.

SLATE

It's difficult to scratch.
Water runs off it.

MARBLE

It looks shiny and pretty.
It can hold heavy weight.

	GRANITE	CHALK	SLATE	MARBLE
STRONG				
CAN BE POLISHED				
SOFT				
HARD				
WATERPROOF				
NOT WATERPROOF				

Rocky — wasn't he a boxer...?

Try to get a look at some rocks in class. Different rock types have different properties.
They don't all do the same thing if you soak them in water or stamp on them.

Uses of Rocks

Rocks are used to make loads of different things.
The type of rock used depends on what properties are needed.

Q1   Oswald has decided to build a castle using chalk, slate, marble and granite.
Fill in the spaces below with the names of rocks — the table on the last page will help.

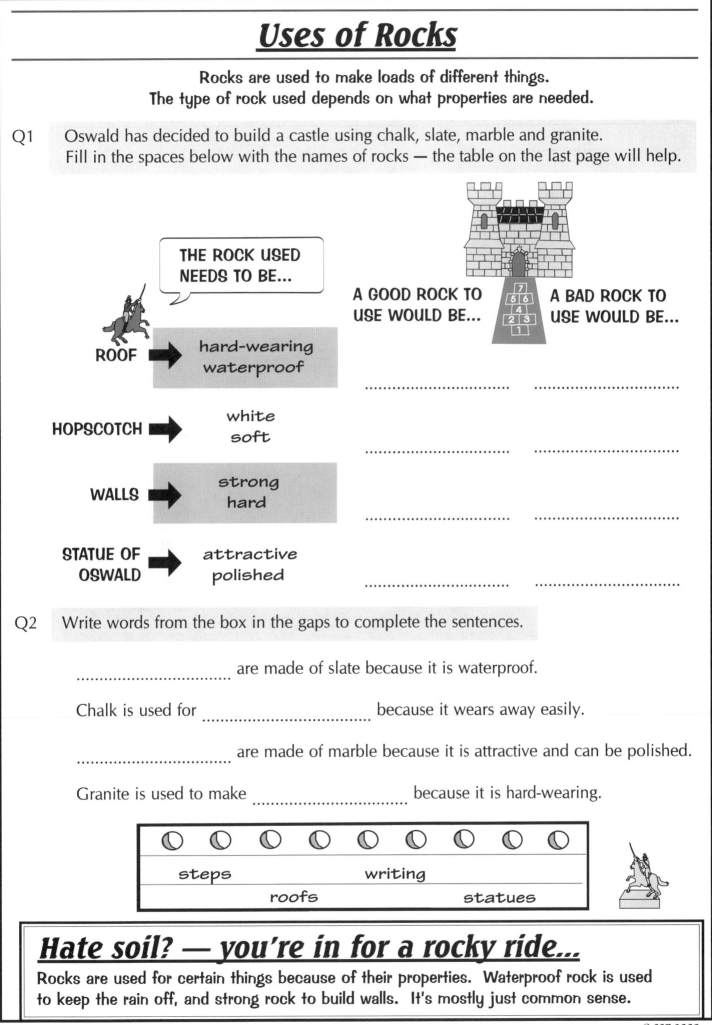

THE ROCK USED
NEEDS TO BE...

A GOOD ROCK TO
USE WOULD BE...

A BAD ROCK TO
USE WOULD BE...

ROOF → hard-wearing
waterproof

....

HOPSCOTCH → white
soft

....

WALLS → strong
hard

....

**STATUE OF
OSWALD** → attractive
polished

....

Q2   Write words from the box in the gaps to complete the sentences.

.... are made of slate because it is waterproof.

Chalk is used for .... because it wears away easily.

.... are made of marble because it is attractive and can be polished.

Granite is used to make .... because it is hard-wearing.

steps	writing
roofs	statues

Hate soil? — you're in for a rocky ride...

Rocks are used for certain things because of their properties. Waterproof rock is used
to keep the rain off, and strong rock to build walls. It's mostly just common sense.

8

Rocks are Everywhere

Rocks are lurking everywhere. The whole world's made of rocks. Well, nearly.

Q1   You can see rocks everywhere. (Circle) all the rocks you can see in these pictures.

on a tropical island

in a churchyard

at the seaside

under the sea

in the countryside

Q2   Fill in the blanks in these sentences about rocks.
Pick the right words from the hat.

slate   noses   rock   cliffs   monkey   houses   dinosaur   sea

Rocks are everywhere.

There are rocks at the bottom of the ....

You can see that .... are made of rock.

Loads of .... are made of stone and use .... for roofs.

The Egyptian pyramids are made of sandstone, which is a type of ....

History Fact:

The Great Pyramid of Khufu in Egypt is made from over 2 million blocks of sandstone. Each block weighs about 2½ tonnes. Must have taken them ages to build it...

Rock-in' all over the world...

If you like cliffs, go to Whitby — it's just awesome. I went once.
Careful though — if you fall off a cliff, it's a long way down...

© CGP 2003

Rocks are Everywhere

Rocks really are <u>everywhere</u>. Underneath everything.
See that grass there — there's rock underneath that.

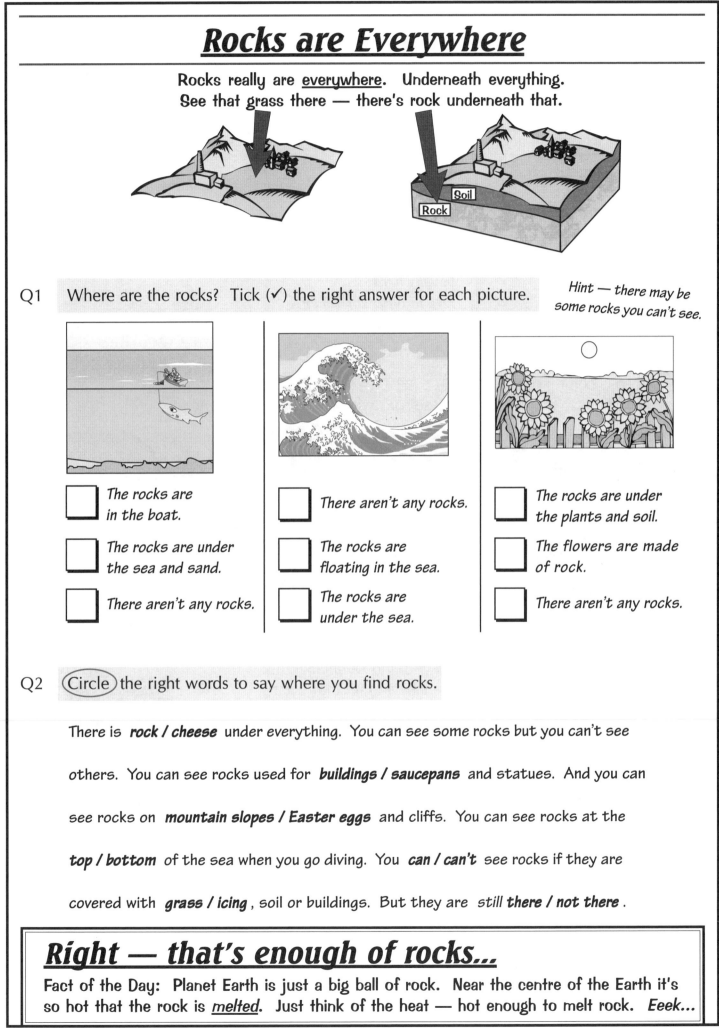

Soil

Rock

Q1 Where are the rocks? Tick (✓) the right answer for each picture.

Hint — there may be some rocks you can't see.

☐ The rocks are in the boat.

☐ The rocks are under the sea and sand.

☐ There aren't any rocks.

☐ There aren't any rocks.

☐ The rocks are floating in the sea.

☐ The rocks are under the sea.

☐ The rocks are under the plants and soil.

☐ The flowers are made of rock.

☐ There aren't any rocks.

Q2 Circle the right words to say where you find rocks.

There is **rock / cheese** under everything. You can see some rocks but you can't see

others. You can see rocks used for **buildings / saucepans** and statues. And you can

see rocks on **mountain slopes / Easter eggs** and cliffs. You can see rocks at the

top / bottom of the sea when you go diving. You **can / can't** see rocks if they are

covered with **grass / icing**, soil or buildings. But they are still **there / not there**.

Right — that's enough of rocks...

Fact of the Day: Planet Earth is just a big ball of rock. Near the centre of the Earth it's
so hot that the rock is <u>melted</u>. Just think of the heat — hot enough to melt rock. **Eeek...**

Soil Comes from Rock

Soil's everywhere — but it didn't get there by chance.
Soil is made when rocks get broken into tiny little pieces.

Q1   These facts are all about rocks and soils. Draw a line from each fact to the right box.

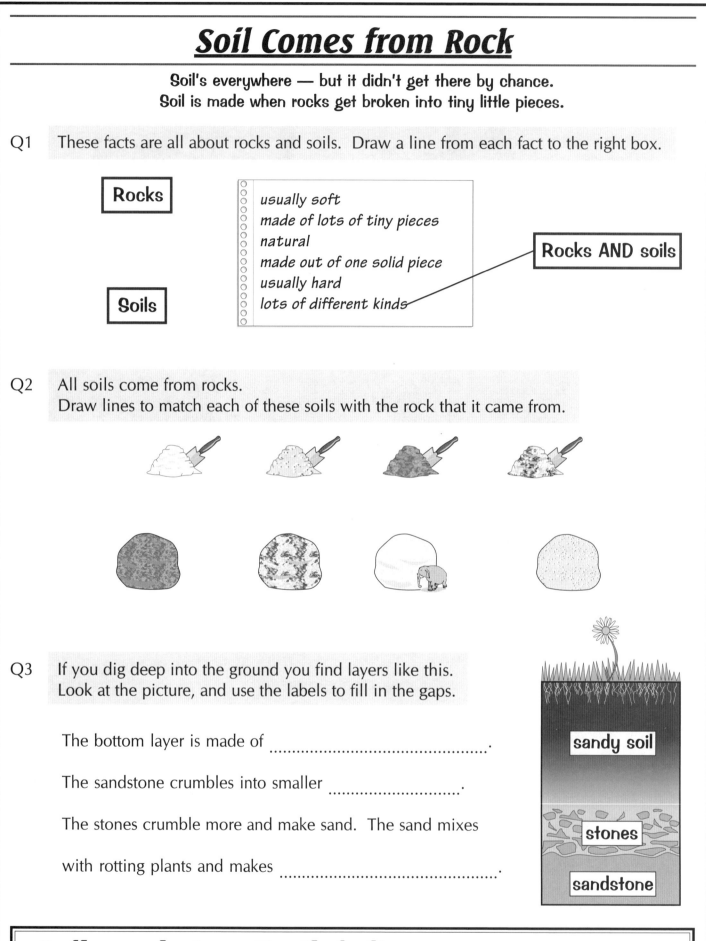

Rocks

- usually soft
- made of lots of tiny pieces
- natural
- made out of one solid piece
- usually hard
- lots of different kinds

Soils

Rocks AND soils

Q2   All soils come from rocks.
Draw lines to match each of these soils with the rock that it came from.

Q3   If you dig deep into the ground you find layers like this.
Look at the picture, and use the labels to fill in the gaps.

The bottom layer is made of ....

The sandstone crumbles into smaller ....

The stones crumble more and make sand. The sand mixes

with rotting plants and makes ....

sandy soil

stones

sandstone

Soil — what on Earth is it...

No more sleepless nights wondering how all that soil came to be lying all over the place.
It's just a lot of tiny bits of rock mixed up with rotten old plants.

Looking at Different Soils

There are loads of different kinds of soil.
The easiest way to tell the difference is by just looking at them.

Q1   Choose words from the box which tell you about each kind of soil.
Write two descriptions under each picture.

soft

hard

dry

wet

lots of stones

lots of roots

lumpy

smooth

sandy

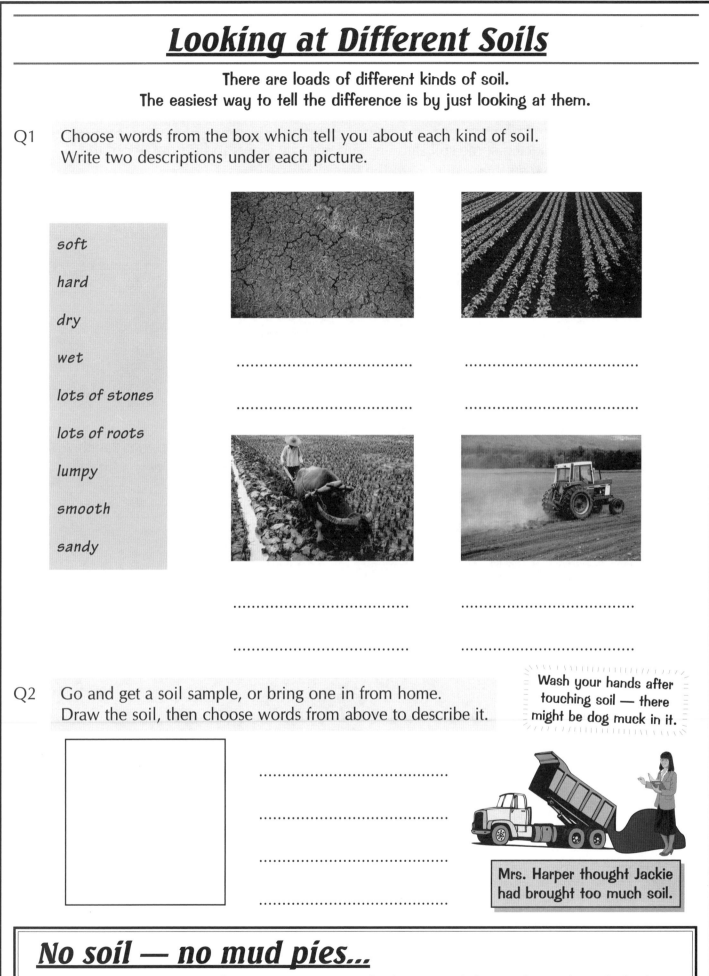

....

....

....

....

Q2   Go and get a soil sample, or bring one in from home.
Draw the soil, then choose words from above to describe it.

Wash your hands after
touching soil — there
might be dog muck in it.

....

....

....

....

Mrs. Harper thought Jackie
had brought too much soil.

No soil — no mud pies...

Soil isn't the same everywhere you go. It can be brown and damp, dry and sandy looking,
nearly black... If you need to describe soil, just say what you see.

Differences in Soils

Looking at soils — great fun. There are some properties of soils
that you can find out just by <u>looking</u> at a sample.

Sancho has collected some soil samples and now he wants to find out about the
differences between them. Here are the samples:

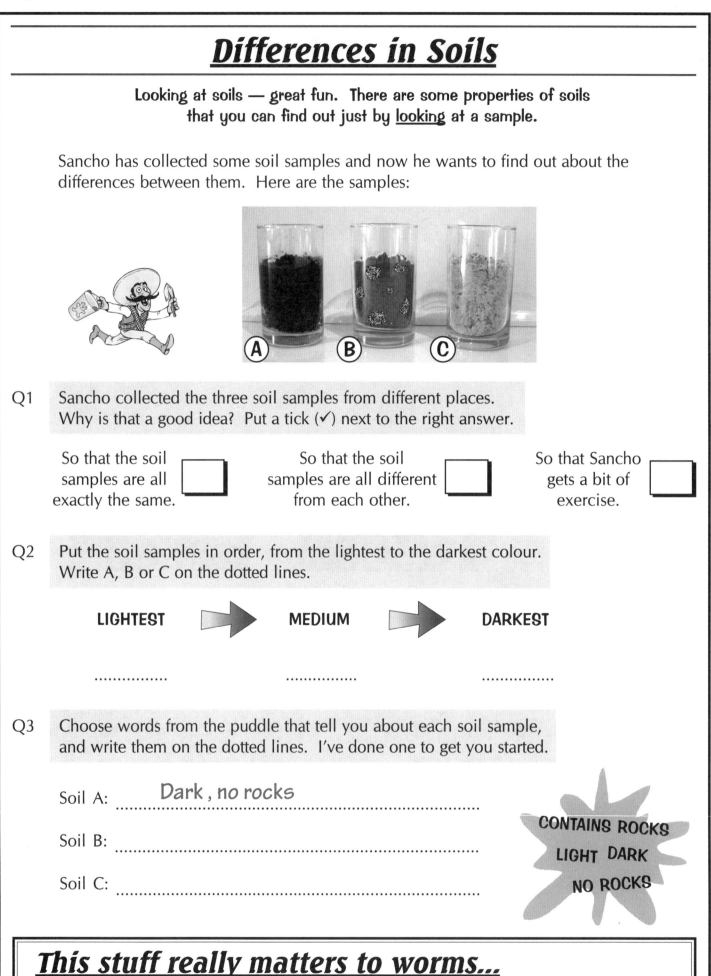

Q1 Sancho collected the three soil samples from different places.
Why is that a good idea? Put a tick (✓) next to the right answer.

So that the soil
samples are all
exactly the same.

So that the soil
samples are all different
from each other.

So that Sancho
gets a bit of
exercise.

Q2 Put the soil samples in order, from the lightest to the darkest colour.
Write A, B or C on the dotted lines.

LIGHTEST ➡ MEDIUM ➡ DARKEST

....

Q3 Choose words from the puddle that tell you about each soil sample,
and write them on the dotted lines. I've done one to get you started.

Soil A: _____Dark , no rocks_____

Soil B: _____

Soil C: _____

CONTAINS ROCKS
LIGHT DARK
NO ROCKS

This stuff really matters to worms...

Okay, maybe you don't want to spend your time looking at soil. I'm not pretending that
soil is really interesting, but you've got to be able to spot differences between samples.

KS2 Science Answers — Rocks and Soils

Q3: LARGE MESH
'If the mesh is large then some particles can go through but the big ones will stay behind' should be circled.

Page 15 Separating Particles from Soil

Q1:

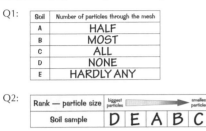

Soil	Number of particles through the mesh
A	HALF
B	MOST
C	ALL
D	NONE
E	HARDLY ANY

Q2:

Rank — particle size	biggest particles ➝ smallest particles
Soil sample	D E A B C

The soil that had the largest particles was sample **D**. You can tell because **no** particles got through the mesh. The soil that had the smallest particles was sample **C**. You can tell because **all** particles got through the mesh.

Page 16 How Does Water Go Through Soils?

Q1: The bottom of the lake is made of **soil**. Water **does not** drain through the soil. School fields are made of **soil**. The water **does** drain through it. Otherwise the school field would turn into a lake.

Q2: Puddle on dry, sandy soil: The puddle has... become a lot smaller.
Puddle on wet, clay soil: The puddle has... stayed the same size.

Q3: The water from the puddles drains away through the **soil**. The water drains more quickly through the **sandy** soil.

Page 17 Measuring Water and Time

Q1: The measuring cylinder should be circled.

Q2: From left to right: 5 cm³, 9 cm³, 10 cm³, 1 cm³.

Q3: The stopwatch should be circled.

Q4: 'Start and stop the timer exactly when you start and stop the investigation' should be ticked.

Page 18 How Quickly Does Water Go Through Soils?

Q1: 'There are different holes so the water will run through at different speeds' should be ticked.

Q2: 'There are different amounts of soil so the water will go through at different speeds' should be ticked.

Page 19 How Quickly Does Water Go Through Soils?

Q1: 'She has added different amounts of water to each container' should be ticked.

Q2: 'Always start timing as soon as she adds the water' should be ticked.

Q3: Jenny's test is **not** a fair test. That means that she won't know if her results are **right**. She needs to keep everything the **same** except the type of soil.

Page 20 Disappearing Puddles

Q1: 'Investigating how much water drains through different soils' should be ticked.

Q2:

Keep the Same Each Time	Change for Each Test	Measure for Each Test
Amount of water poured onto soil	Type of soil used	Amount of water collected from soil
Amount of soil used		
Size of holes in pot		
Length of time		
Size of container		

Page 21 Disappearing Puddles

Q1: There's lots you could write. Here's my plan for the investigation:
Title: Investigating how much water drains through different soils.
Equipment: 5 different samples of soil, measuring cylinder, stopwatch, cups with holes in them, a plastic tray, paper and pencil.

Method 1:

Water is poured onto each soil

Time how long water takes to go through

Water is collected and measured

(repeated for each soil)
2: For each soil I will start the stopwatch as soon as I pour 50 ml of water onto it. After 1 minute I will stop the stopwatch.
3: For each soil I will measure the amount of water that has collected in the plastic tray after 1 minute.
4: I will use the same amount of water each time. I will also start and stop the stopwatch at the same point each time.

Page 22 Disappearing Puddles

Q1: Depends on your results. I've used the sample data from the bottom of the page:

	Soil A	Soil B	Soil C	Soil D	Soil E
Amount of water collected from soil (in ml)	16	44	5	23	33

Q2:

Page 23 Disappearing Puddles

Q1: Here's the table for my sample data:

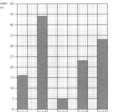

	Soil A	Soil B	Soil C	Soil D	Soil E
Is it sandy?	✗	✓	✗	✗	✓
Is it a clay soil?	✓	✗	✓	✓	✗
Does it have loads of stones in it?	✓	✗	✓	✓	?
Does it have loads of gaps in it?	?	✓	✗	✓	✓
Does it have loads of rotting leaves in it?	✗	✗	✓	?	✓

Q2: Sample data: 1. Soil B   2. Soil E   3. Soil D   4. Soil A   5. Soil C

Q3: Water goes quickest through sandy soil with big gaps. It goes quickest if there are no stones or leaves in the soil.

Page 24 Revision Questions

Q1: The rocks have been grouped by **colour**.
'By size' and 'by smoothness' should be circled.

Q2: The **white** rock is the hardest. You know because bits are coming off the **black** rock.

Q3: Slate: waterproof   Chalk: soft   Granite: building walls

Q4: **Rocks** are everywhere — under sand and soil and at the bottom of the sea. In fact the Earth is a big ball of **rock**.

Page 25 Revision Questions

Q5: **Rock** breaks up into little pieces.
These little pieces mix with **rotting plants** to make soil.

Q6: Sandy and dry — A   Dark and stony — C   Dark and wet — B

Q7: Only particles **A** and **D** can go through the mesh. Particles **B** and **C** will stay behind. This trick can be used to **separate** out large particles.

Q8: Water goes through some soils **quicker** than others. If you want to investigate this it is important to change the type of soil and keep everything else the **same**. This method of keeping everything the same is called making it a **fair test**.

Marble floor tiles can be polished.

soil

rock

From the CGP KS2 Science Book — Rocks and Soils

KS2 Science Answers — Rocks and Soils

Page 1 Background

Q1: Very hard and usually white. Can be polished. — **Marble**
Grey and quite smooth. Easily splits into thin layers. — **Slate**
Light-coloured and very heavy. Rough to touch. — **Granite**

Q2: Brick — **man-made** Granite — **natural**
Concrete slab — **man-made** Marble — **natural**

Q3: Roof: slate; walls: brick; pretty statue in the garden: marble

Page 2 Grouping Rocks

Q1: 'Size of pebble' should be ticked.

Q2: Because it is smooth and has the same pattern on it.

Page 3 Grouping Rocks

Q1: a) 'Size of particles' should be ticked.
b) Group B

Q2: a) The second and third rocks should be ticked.
b) Because you can see the layers in the rocks. You can see fossils in the third rock too.

Page 4 Wearing Rocks Away

Q1: a) The **black** rock is softer than the **white** rock.
  BLACK (softer)
  WHITE (harder)
b) The **white** rock is softer than the **light grey** rock.
  BLACK (softer)
  WHITE
  LIGHT GREY (harder)
c) The **dark grey** rock is softer than the **black** rock.
  DARK GREY (softer)
  BLACK
  WHITE
  LIGHT GREY (harder)

Page 5 Rocks and Water

Q1: a)

Rock	B	D	C	A
Time for water to soak in, in seconds	10	35	105	didn't go in

b) Water soaks into some rocks more **quickly** than others. In this test, the water soaked into rock **B** the quickest, and into rock **C** the slowest. The water didn't go into rock **A** at all. If **water** goes into a rock easily, you say that the rock is 'absorbent'.

Page 6 Properties of Rocks

Q1: Granite: 'strong' and 'hard' should be ticked.
Chalk: 'soft' and 'not waterproof' should be ticked.
Slate: 'hard' and 'waterproof' should be ticked.
Marble: 'can be polished' and 'strong' should be ticked.

Page 7 Uses of Rocks

Q1: Roof: Good rock — slate. Bad rock — chalk.
Hopscotch: Good rock — chalk. Bad rock — slate, marble, granite.
Walls: Good rock — granite, marble, slate. Bad rock — chalk
Statue: Good rock — marble. Bad rock — chalk, slate.

Q2: **Roofs** are made of slate because it is waterproof. Chalk is used for **writing** because it wears away easily. **Statues** are made of marble because it is attractive and can be polished. Granite is used to make **steps** because it is hard-wearing.

Page 8 Rocks are Everywhere

Q1:

Q2: Rocks are everywhere. There are rocks at the bottom of the **sea**. You can see that **cliffs** are made of rock. Loads of **houses** are made of stone and use **slate** for roofs. The Egyptian pyramids are made of sandstone, which is a type of **rock**.

Page 9 Rocks are Everywhere

Q1: First picture: 'The rocks are under the sea and sand' should be ticked.
Second picture: 'The rocks are under the sea' should be ticked.
Third picture: 'The rocks are under the plants and soil' should be ticked.

Q2: There is **rock** under everything. You can see some rocks but you can't see others. You can see rocks used for **buildings** and statues. And you can see rocks on **mountain slopes** and cliffs. You can see rocks at the **bottom** of the sea when you go diving. You **can't** see rocks if they are covered with **grass**, soil or buildings. But they are **still there**.

Page 10 Soil Comes from Rock

Q1: Rocks — made out of one solid piece, usually hard
Soils — usually soft, made out of lots of tiny pieces
Rocks AND soils — natural

Q2: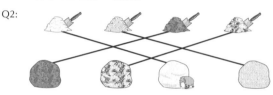

Q3: The bottom layer is made of **sandstone**. The sandstone crumbles into smaller **stones**. The stones crumble more and make sand. The sand mixes with rotting plants and makes **sandy soil**.

Page 11 Looking at Different Soils

Q1: Any two of these answers for each soil would be correct.
Top left: hard, dry, lots of roots
Top right: soft, wet, lumpy
Bottom left: soft, wet, lumpy
Bottom right: dry, lots of stones, smooth, sandy

Q2: Depends on the type of soil you're looking at. Here's my soil:

 Sandy, lots of stones, dry, soft, smooth.

Page 12 Differences in Soils

Q1: 'So that the soil samples are all different from each other' should be ticked.

Q2: Lightest — C, medium — B, darkest — A

Q3: Soil B: Contains rocks, dark.
Soil C: Light, no rocks.

Page 13 Differences in Soils

Q1: Soil A: ALL SMALL PARTICLES
Soil B: SOME LARGE PARTICLES
Soil C: SOME LARGE PARTICLES

Q2: NO

Q3: You can't tell exactly what **size** the particles are just by looking at them. It's hard to tell whether the particles are bigger in sample B or sample **C**. You need to **measure** the particles somehow.

Page 14 Separating Particles from Soil

Q1: It's hard to tell how **big** soil particles are just by **looking** at them. Using a **sieve** is the best way of separating big particles from soil. Then you can see **how many** particles get through the sieve.

Q2: Only particles **B** and **C** can go through the mesh. Particles **A** and **D** will stay behind.

Differences in Soils

The colour and wetness of soil aren't the only things to look out for.
The pieces that <u>make up</u> the soil can be different sizes. These pieces are called <u>particles</u>.

Now Sancho has collected three new soil samples. He wants to investigate the size of
the particles that make up the soils. Here are his samples:

A   B   C

Q1   Take a look at the soil samples — then write
ALL SMALL PARTICLES or SOME LARGE PARTICLES
on the dotted line for each sample.

Soil A: ....

Soil B: ....

Soil C: ....

Q2   Can you put the soil samples in order of particle size?
Write YES or NO on the dotted line.

....

Q3   What is the problem with looking at particle size in soils?
Circle the right words to finish off these sentences.

You can't tell exactly what **COLOUR / SIZE** the particles are just by looking at them.

It's hard to tell whether the particles are bigger in sample B or sample **A / C** .

You need to **COUNT / MEASURE** the particles somehow.

Sancho took his
search for the best
soil a bit too far.

Who'd have thought soils were so much fun...

Looking at soils is fine, but there are some things that you can't tell just by looking.
The next page is about how to test for properties that are harder to spot.

Separating Particles from Soil

There's a good way to separate big particles from soil to see how big they really are.
This page is all about how to do it.

Q1 Fill in the gaps in these sentences about separating
particles from soil. Use words from the wiggly grey box.

It's hard to tell how .... soil particles are

just by .... at them. Using a

.... is the best way of separating big

particles from soil. Then you can see

.... particles get through the sieve.

> HOW MANY
> HAT
> POINTING   BIG
> LOOKING   SIEVE

Q2 Sancho is using a sieve to separate out the large particles.
The picture below shows a close up of particles in a sieve mesh.
Fill in the gaps in these sentences with the right letters.

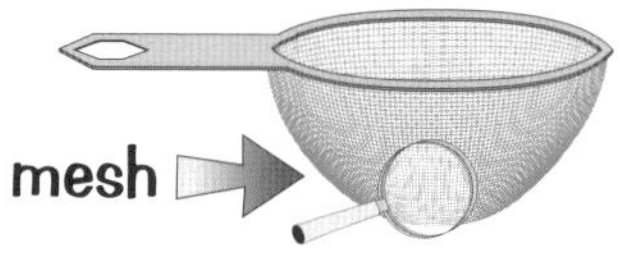

mesh →

Only particles .... and .... can go

through the mesh. Particles .... and

.... will stay behind.

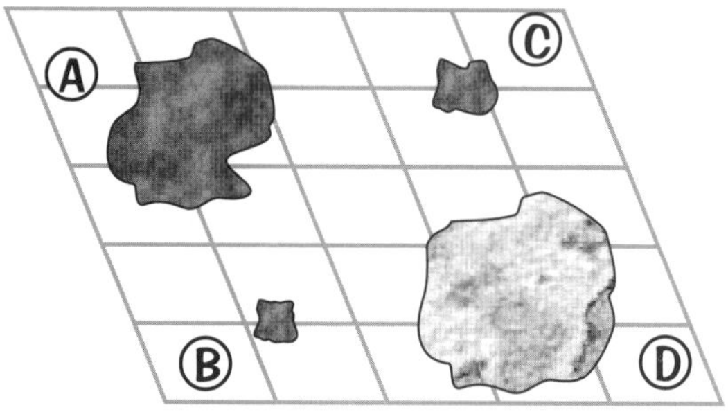

Q3 What kind of mesh should Sancho's sieve have? Write LARGE MESH
or SMALL MESH on the dotted line — then circle the reason why.

(Hint: A large mesh means
the sieve has big holes.)

....

The mesh should be
small so that none of the
particles can go through.

The mesh should be **large** so some
particles can go through but the
big ones will stay behind.

Don't worry — there's another fun page left...

OK, so using a sieve is the best way to separate particles. Pretty useful, huh.
On the next page you can see some sieves in action.

Separating Particles from Soil

Sancho is using a sieve to separate some different soils.
The soils are all dry and he used the same sieve each time to keep it a __fair test__.

Q1   Look at the diagram below showing the results of Sancho's sieving investigation.
Then fill in the table using the words in the jagged grey box.

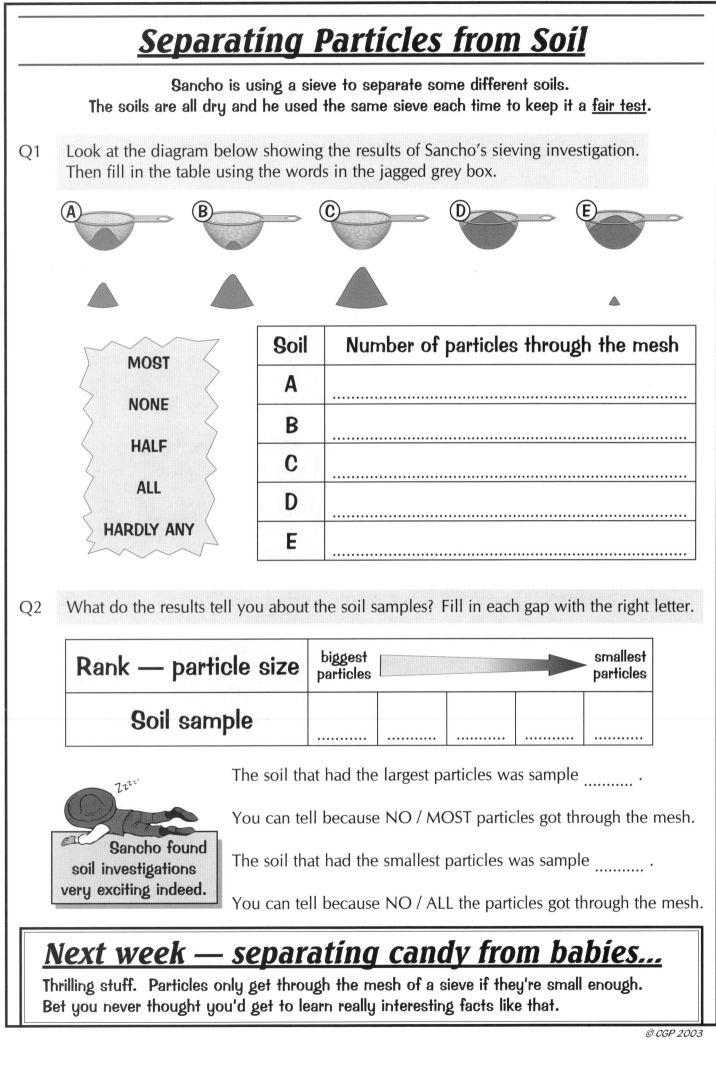

Words in box:

MOST

NONE

HALF

ALL

HARDLY ANY

Soil	Number of particles through the mesh
A	....
B	....
C	....
D	....
E	....

Q2   What do the results tell you about the soil samples? Fill in each gap with the right letter.

Rank — particle size	biggest particles				smallest particles
Soil sample	....	....	....	....	....

The soil that had the largest particles was sample ....

You can tell because NO / MOST particles got through the mesh.

The soil that had the smallest particles was sample ....

Sancho found soil investigations very exciting indeed.

You can tell because NO / ALL the particles got through the mesh.

Next week — separating candy from babies...

Thrilling stuff. Particles only get through the mesh of a sieve if they're small enough.
Bet you never thought you'd get to learn really interesting facts like that.

How Does Water Go Through Soils?

When it rains you get puddles. Some puddles disappear
quickly but others hang around for ages.

Q1 Choose the correct words from the puddle and write them in the gaps.

The bottom of the lake is

made of ....

Water .... drain through the soil.

does not *feathers* *soil* *does* *soil* *ducks*

School fields are made of ....

The water .... drain through it.

Otherwise the school field could turn into a lake.

Q2 Look at these pictures of puddles on different types of soil. Fill in the
gaps to say what has happened to the **size** of the puddles after a while.

At first

A puddle on
dry, sandy
soil.

Later

The puddle has...

....

....

....

At first

A puddle on
wet, clay
soil.

Later

The puddle has...

....

....

....

Q3 Fill in the gaps to explain what has happened in the pictures in Q2.

The water from puddles usually drains away through the .... [soil / sky].

The water drains more quickly through the .... [sandy / clay] soil.

I'm getting in a big puddle...

Water goes through some soils more quickly than others — simple as that.

Measuring Water and Time

In the next few pages there's all sorts of experiments to see how quickly water goes through soil. But to do them you need to measure water and time accurately.

Q1 (Circle) the best thing to measure how much water to add to the soil.

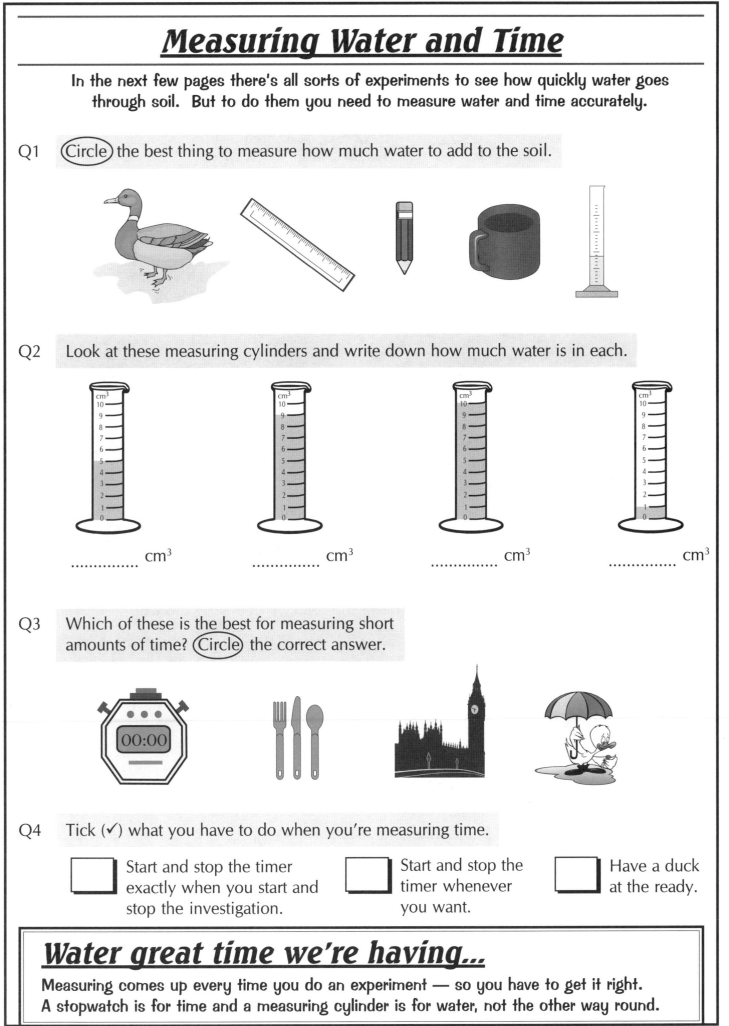

Q2 Look at these measuring cylinders and write down how much water is in each.

.... cm³   .... cm³   .... cm³   .... cm³

Q3 Which of these is the best for measuring short amounts of time? (Circle) the correct answer.

Q4 Tick (✓) what you have to do when you're measuring time.

☐ Start and stop the timer exactly when you start and stop the investigation.

☐ Start and stop the timer whenever you want.

☐ Have a duck at the ready.

Water great time we're having...

Measuring comes up every time you do an experiment — so you have to get it right. A stopwatch is for time and a measuring cylinder is for water, not the other way round.

How Quickly Does Water Go Through Soils?

Jenny is doing an experiment about how quickly water goes through different types of soil...

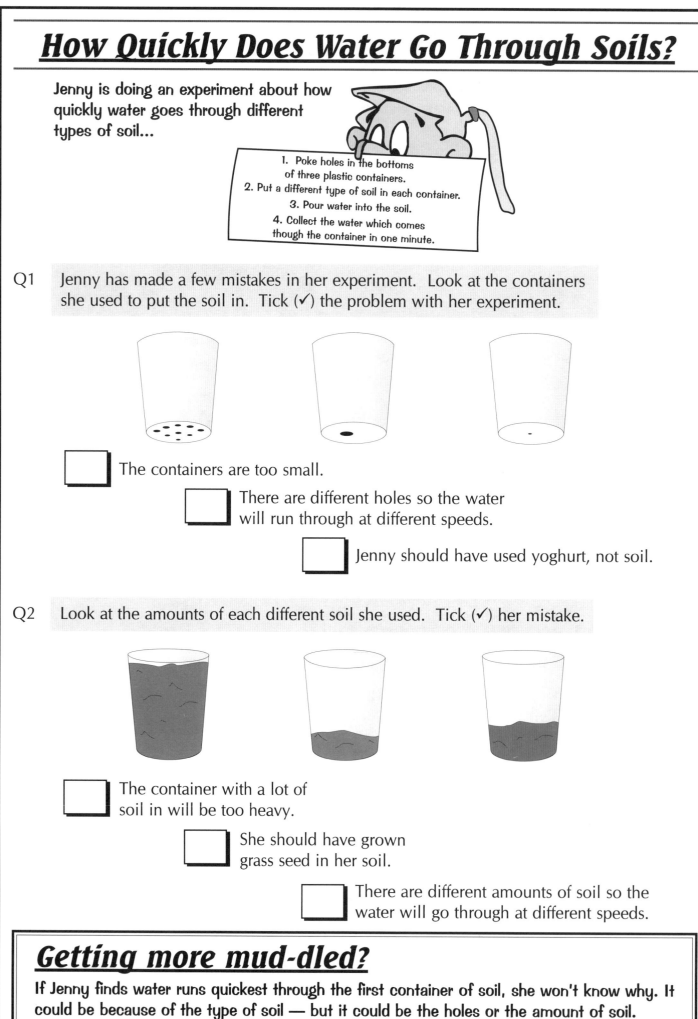

1. Poke holes in the bottoms of three plastic containers.
2. Put a different type of soil in each container.
3. Pour water into the soil.
4. Collect the water which comes though the container in one minute.

Q1   Jenny has made a few mistakes in her experiment. Look at the containers she used to put the soil in. Tick (✓) the problem with her experiment.

☐ The containers are too small.

☐ There are different holes so the water will run through at different speeds.

☐ Jenny should have used yoghurt, not soil.

Q2   Look at the amounts of each different soil she used. Tick (✓) her mistake.

☐ The container with a lot of soil in will be too heavy.

☐ She should have grown grass seed in her soil.

☐ There are different amounts of soil so the water will go through at different speeds.

Getting more mud-dled?

If Jenny finds water runs quickest through the first container of soil, she won't know why. It could be because of the type of soil — but it could be the holes or the amount of soil.

How Quickly Does Water Go Through Soils?

Another page of Jenny's mistakes I'm afraid.

Q1 Look at the three cylinders to show how much water Jenny added
to each container. Tick (✓) the problem with her experiment.

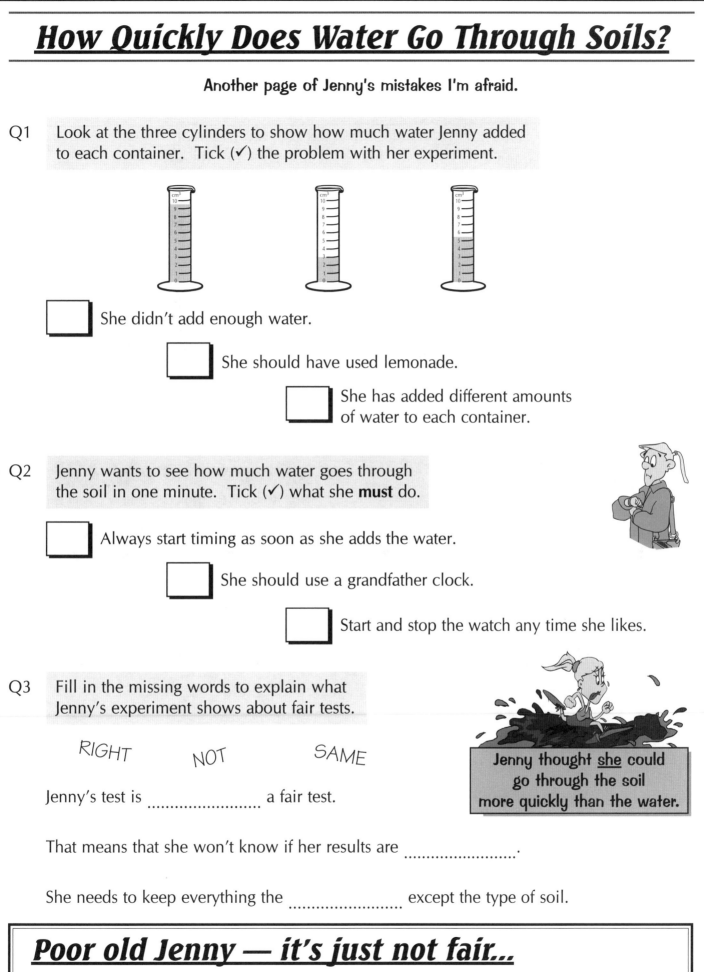

☐ She didn't add enough water.

☐ She should have used lemonade.

☐ She has added different amounts
of water to each container.

Q2 Jenny wants to see how much water goes through
the soil in one minute. Tick (✓) what she **must** do.

☐ Always start timing as soon as she adds the water.

☐ She should use a grandfather clock.

☐ Start and stop the watch any time she likes.

Q3 Fill in the missing words to explain what
Jenny's experiment shows about fair tests.

RIGHT   NOT   SAME

Jenny's test is .... a fair test.

That means that she won't know if her results are ....

She needs to keep everything the .... except the type of soil.

> Jenny thought <u>she</u> could
> go through the soil
> more quickly than the water.

Poor old Jenny — it's just not fair...

The important thing to remember when doing an experiment is to make it a fair test. If you
want to find out about different types of soil you MUST keep everything else the same.

MINI-PROJECT

Disappearing Puddles

Inspector Gorse has loads of puddles in his garden.
He notices that the puddles drain away quicker through some soils than others.

Q1 Inspector Gorse wants an investigation. He wants to know what is happening.
What would be a good name for the investigation? Tick (✓) the best name.

☐ Adventures with Mud

☐ Investigating how much water drains through different soils

☐ Investigating how much soil there is in the garden

☐ Investigating how well different soils float on water

☐ Larry Potter and the Philosopher's Soil

Inspector Gorse wants YOU to find out what's going on.
He gives you this equipment:

You also need to collect 5 different
soil samples. Label them Soils A to E.

Soil A Soil B Soil C Soil D Soil E

On pages 18 and 19 Jenny did a similar investigation. Her test wasn't fair — but
Inspector Gorse wants <u>this</u> test to be fair. If it's not fair, the results will be no good.

Q2 Fill in the table to say how you can make the test fair.
Say what to keep the same, what to change and what to measure.

Keep the Same Each Time	Change for Each Test	Measure for Each Test
Amount of water poured onto soil		
Length of time		
Size of container		

Type of soil used   Amount of soil used

Size of holes in pot   Amount of water collected from soil

Mud — glorious mud...

BE CAREFUL when you collect soils. Keep away from broken glass or
rusty cans — and ALWAYS WASH YOUR HANDS afterwards.

Whoops.

Disappearing Puddles

MINI-PROJECT

Use this page to plan your investigation. Fill in all the gaps.
(I've started filling in some of the gaps for you.)

Title: ....

Equipment:

5 different samples of soil
....

....

....

Method:

1. Draw a picture of the experiment:

Label your drawing to make it clear.

2. Explain what you're going to do: For each soil I will...

....

....

Say what you'll actually DO with the equipment.

3. Say what you are going to measure: For each soil I will measure...

....

4. Say how you will make sure it's a fair test: I will use the same amount

of water each time. I will also...

....

....

Planning — the fun never stops...

*plan...
must... plan...*

All scientists plan an experiment before they do it. It's true — even Einstein did it.

© CGP 2003

MINI-PROJECT

Disappearing Puddles

Do the experiment.

Q1   Do the experiment and write your results in this table.   [If you can't do the experiment, you can use my results at the bottom of the page.]

If you measured something different, cross this out and write in what you measured.

	Soil A	Soil B	Soil C	Soil D	Soil E
Amount of water collected from soil (in ml)					

Q2   Draw a bar chart of your results here:

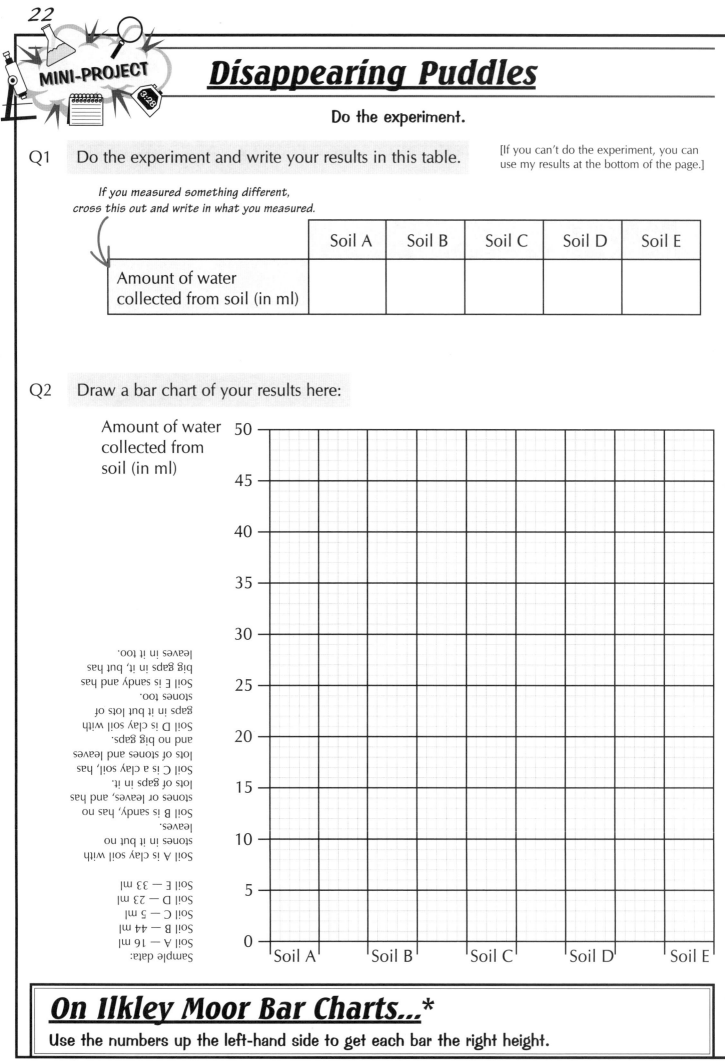

Amount of water collected from soil (in ml)

Sample data:
Soil A — 16 ml
Soil B — 44 ml
Soil C — 5 ml
Soil D — 23 ml
Soil E — 33 ml

Soil A is clay soil with stones in it but no leaves.
Soil B is sandy, has no stones or leaves, and has lots of gaps in it.
Soil C is a clay soil, has lots of stones and leaves and no big gaps.
Soil D is clay soil with gaps in it but lots of stones too.
Soil E is sandy and has big gaps in it, but has leaves in it too.

On Ilkley Moor Bar Charts...*

Use the numbers up the left-hand side to get each bar the right height.

* It's alright, you don't have to laugh.

Disappearing Puddles

Inspector Gorse wants more than just results. He wants conclusions.
Answer these questions then make a conclusion from your investigation.

Q1   Describe the soils in your investigation. Fill in this table.
       Put a tick (✓) or a cross (✗) or a question mark (?) in each box.

Don't tick both "clay" and "sandy" for the same soil — that would be silly.

	Soil A	Soil B	Soil C	Soil D	Soil E
Is it sandy?					
Is it a clay soil?					
Does it have loads of stones in it?					
Does it have loads of gaps in it?					
Does it have loads of rotting leaves in it?					

Q2   Look at the bar chart. Put the soils in order of how much water they let through.

Most water flowed through the soil

1.   ....

2.   ....

3.   ....

4.   ....

5.   ....

Least water flowed through the soil

Sam's puddle was disappearing quicker than he expected...

Q3   Write a conclusion about the investigation. Say which soils let the
       most and **least** water through — and **say why** you think this was.

Look back at your answers to Q1 and Q2.

....

....

Result of my investigation — the butler did it...

Conclusions can seem pointless if the results are obvious to you. But you still need to say
what you found out — and what it means. Then it's obvious to everyone else too.

Revision Questions

Hold on to your hats, two solid pages of revision questions — rock on...

Q1   These rocks are in groups. Fill in the missing word to say how they've been grouped.

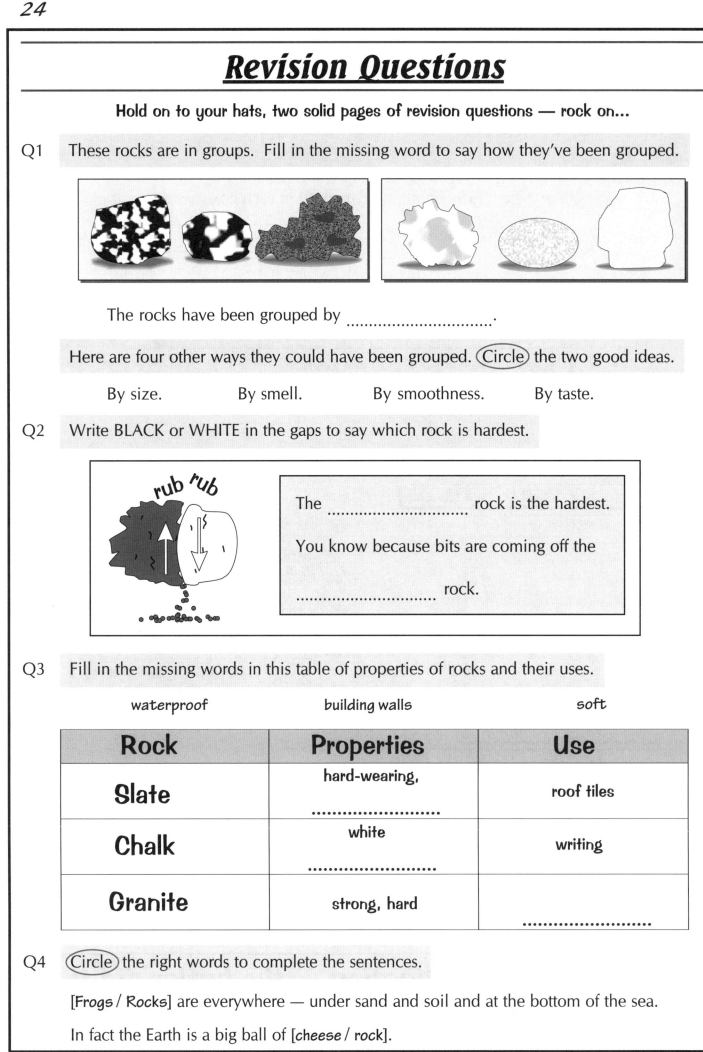

The rocks have been grouped by ....:

Here are four other ways they could have been grouped. Circle the two good ideas.

By size.   By smell.   By smoothness.   By taste.

Q2   Write BLACK or WHITE in the gaps to say which rock is hardest.

rub rub

The .... rock is the hardest.

You know because bits are coming off the

.... rock.

Q3   Fill in the missing words in this table of properties of rocks and their uses.

waterproof   building walls   soft

Rock	Properties	Use
Slate	hard-wearing, ...	roof tiles
Chalk	white	writing
Granite	strong, hard	....

Q4   Circle the right words to complete the sentences.

[Frogs / Rocks] are everywhere — under sand and soil and at the bottom of the sea.

In fact the Earth is a big ball of [cheese / rock].

Revision Questions

That's rocks done, now for soil — it's just fun fun fun at school these days...

Q5 (Circle) the correct words to describe where soil comes from.

[Mud / Rock] breaks up into little pieces.

These little pieces mix with [lemonade / rotting plants] to make soil.

Q6 Write the letters in the boxes to match the soil samples to their descriptions.

Sample A 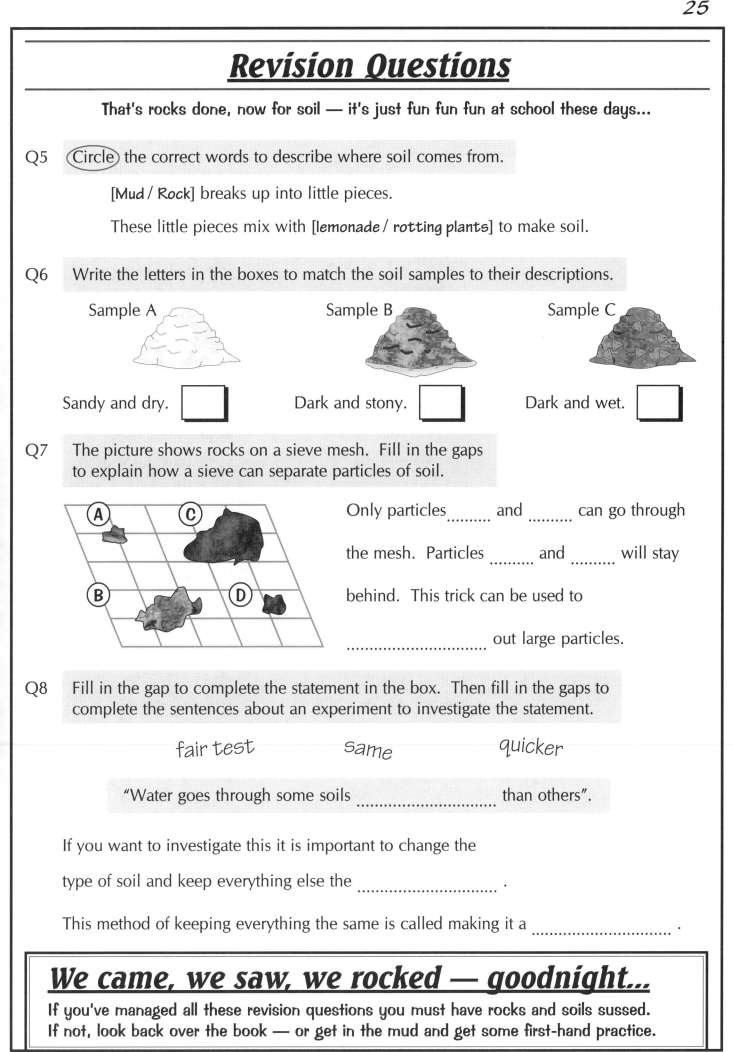   Sample B   Sample C

Sandy and dry. ☐   Dark and stony. ☐   Dark and wet. ☐

Q7 The picture shows rocks on a sieve mesh. Fill in the gaps to explain how a sieve can separate particles of soil.

Only particles .... and .... can go through

the mesh. Particles .... and .... will stay

behind. This trick can be used to

.... out large particles.

Q8 Fill in the gap to complete the statement in the box. Then fill in the gaps to complete the sentences about an experiment to investigate the statement.

fair test   same   quicker

"Water goes through some soils .... than others".

If you want to investigate this it is important to change the

type of soil and keep everything else the ....

This method of keeping everything the same is called making it a ....

We came, we saw, we rocked — goodnight...

If you've managed all these revision questions you must have rocks and soils sussed.
If not, look back over the book — or get in the mud and get some first-hand practice.

Index

A
absorbent 5

B
bar charts 22

C
chalk 6, 7
colour of rocks 2, 3
colour of soils 10-13
conclusions 23
concrete 1
crumbling rocks 6, 7

D
dead plants 3, 10
diamonds 4
dinosaurs 3
disappearing puddles 16, 20-23
dog muck 11
dripping water onto rocks 5
dry soil 11-13
ducks 17

E
Earth 9
Egyptian pyramids 8
Einstein 21
experiments 16-23

F
fair tests 15, 18-20
fossils 3

G
granite 1, 6, 7
grouping rocks 2, 3

H
hardness 1, 4, 11
heavy weights 6, 7
holes in cups 18, 19

I
index 26 (obviously)
Inspector Gorse 20-23
investigations 16-23

L
lakes 16
Larry Potter 20
layers of rock 3
layers of soil 10

M
man-made 1
marble 1, 6, 7
measuring cylinders 17, 19
measuring time 17, 19
measuring particle size 13-15
measuring water 17, 19
melted rock 9
meshes 14, 15
monsters 5
Mr Quiff 2
mud pies 11

P
particles 3, 13-15
planning investigations 21
polishing stones 1, 6, 7
pretty rocks 6, 7
properties 1, 4, 6, 7, 12-15
puddles 16, 20-23
pyramids 8

R
results tables 5, 20, 22, 23
revision questions 24, 25
rock groups 2, 3
rocks are everywhere 8, 9
roofs 1, 7
rubbing rocks together 4

S
sandstone 10
school fields 16
scratching rocks 6, 7
sea 8, 9
sedimentary rocks 3
separating particles from soils 14, 15
sieves 14, 15
size of particles 3, 14, 15
size of rocks 2, 3
slate 1, 5-7
smoothness 1-3, 6, 7
softness 4, 11
soil 9-23
statues 1, 7, 9
stopwatches 17

W
walls 1, 7
waterproof 6, 7
water going through soils 16-23
water soaking into rocks 5-7
wearing rocks away 4
wet soil 11-13
Whitby 8
writing with chalk 7